Humans and Other Animals
Senses

David and Penny Glover

FRANKLIN WATTS
LONDON • SYDNEY

First published in 2004 by
Franklin Watts
338 Euston Road
London NW1 3BH

Franklin Watts Australia
Level 17/207 Kent Street
Sydney, NSW 2000

Series Editor: Sally Luck
Art Director: Jonathan Hair
Design: Matthew Lilly

ISBN 978 0 7496 5544 0

All photographs taken by Ray Moller unless
otherwise credited.

Acknowledgements: R Austing/FLPA: front
cover r, 11c; G J Cambridge/NHPA: 21b;
James Carmichael Jr/NHPA: 9br; Phillip
Colla/Ecoscene: 13l; Manfred
Danegger/NHPA: 7tr; Delpho/Still Pictures:
11b; Reinhard Dirsheri/Ecoscene: 25t; Clive
Druett/Ecoscene: 21t; Pierre Gleizes/Still
Pictures: 19t; Roger de la Harpe/Still Pictures:
9t; Martin Harvey/NHPA: 23b.
David Lucas (www.dclvisions.com): 18;
Brian Mitchell/Photofusion: 14t, 16;
B.Odeur/Still Pictures: 13r; Robert
Pickett/Ecoscene: 7tl, 17t, 19b;
F Ravendam/Minden/FLPA: 17b; Jeffrey
Rotman/Still Pictures: 23t; Roland Seitre/Still
Pictures: 7b; Albert Visage/Still Pictures: 15b,
25b; Konrad Wothe/Minden/FLPA: 15t.

Every attempt has been made to clear
copyright. Should there be any inadvertent
omission, please apply to the publisher for
rectification

A CIP catalogue record for this book is
available from the British Library.

Printed in China

Franklin Watts is a division of Hachette
Children's Books.

Contents

What are the senses?

Our five senses are
smelling, tasting, feeling, hearing
and seeing.

We use our senses to explore the world around us.

Open a cold fizzy drink.
Can you see it?
Hear it? Feel it?
Smell it? Taste it?

Like humans, other animals use their senses to explore. A hungry fox smells a rabbit, then sees it in the grass. The rabbit hears the fox, and stamps a warning to other rabbits.

A kiwi has tiny eyes so it cannot see very well. To find food, it pokes the ground with its long bill. Its bill helps it to smell worms and feel them move.

How do we see?

We see with our eyes.

Humans have two eyes. They are on our face, so we can see in front of us and a little to the side. We have to turn our heads and bodies to see around us.

Like a human, a crocodile has two eyes, but they are on top of its head. The crocodile can see above the water as it swims towards its prey.

Hold up a finger and look at it. Shut one eye at a time. Does the finger move? Two eyes help us to see where things are.

Some animals have more than two eyes. This spider has 8 eyes: 2 main eyes at the front look for food. The other eyes look around for danger - like a hungry lizard or bird!

Can we see in the dark?

No.
We need light to see.

At night the sky grows dark. Outside, the moon and stars give us a little light, but we also use street lamps and torches to help us see. Inside, we put on electric lights.

Look in the mirror.
Close your eyes.
Your pupils get bigger
in the dark. Now open your
eyes and watch them get small again!

An owl has powerful eyes.
It hunts at night and can
see small animals in the
grass. If we had eyes like
owls, they would be as big
as tennis balls!

A mole has
tiny eyes. Like
humans, it cannot
see in the dark.
It finds its way
underground by
touch and smell.

How do we hear?

We hear with our ears.

Sounds are all around us. We have two ears to help us tell where sounds come from. Our ears help us to dance along to music!

Close your eyes and listen. Hold up a finger each time you hear a different sound. Can you count ten sounds?

The blue whale is the biggest animal in the world. It sings underwater to talk to other whales. Blue whales can hear each other singing hundreds of kilometres away!

Bats use their ears to hunt in the dark. They make clicking sounds which bounce back to them from other animals, like moths. When they hear these echoes, they can catch their prey.

Can we all hear the same sounds?

No. We do not all hear the same sounds.

Some people have good hearing, but others cannot hear well. They talk using their hands. This is called sign language.

We use sign language when we wave hello or goodbye. What other signs do you use? Can you learn some new ones?

Snails do not have ears so they cannot hear. They use their other senses to find food and keep safe.

An aardvark has very large ears. Its hearing is so good that it can hear ants walking underground. It listens carefully, then digs the ants out and eats them up!

How do we feel?

We feel with
our skin.

Our skin feels if
something is hard
or soft, rough or
smooth, wet or dry.
Fingertips are very
sensitive. This
girl is blind. She
can read
braille. She
feels the
letters with
her fingertips.

Cut out the letters in your name from sandpaper. Jumble them up. Put on a blindfold. Can you make your name by touch?

Some animals feel with special body parts. A cat has whiskers. Whiskers help it to feel its way in the dark.

A sea anemone looks like a plant but it is an animal. It feels with its tentacles. When a small fish touches them, the sea anemone stings it, drags it to its mouth and eats it.

17

Can we feel heat?

Yes. Our skin feels if something is hot or cold.

The water in a baby's bath must not be too hot, or too cold. An adult tests the water first and puts the baby in when it feels just right.

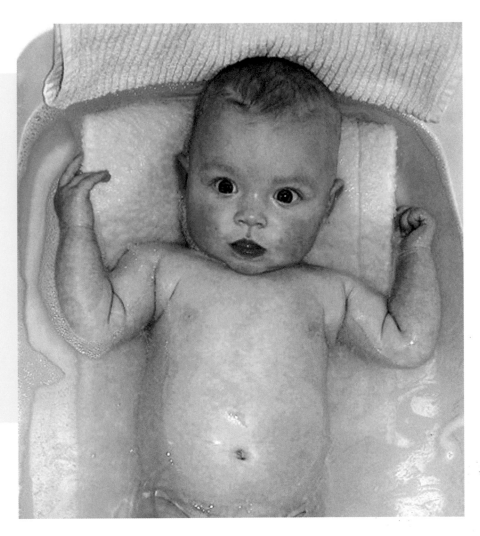

How long does it take you to get used to a cold swimming pool? Does it feel different when you get out, then get back in again?

Seals do not feel
cold on icy land.
Thick layers of fat
and fur keep their
bodies warm.

Some snakes have special
pits in the skin under their
eyes. The pits can sense the
warmth of a nearby mouse.
This helps the snakes to
hunt in the dark.

How do we smell?

We smell with our noses.

We breathe in through our nose to sniff smells. Smells can be good or bad. We enjoy good smells, but bad smells can warn us of danger.

What smells do you like? What smells don't you like? Ask your friends and make a 'Smell Top Ten'.

Bears have long noses. This means they can smell better than humans can. A bear can smell honey from over 5 kilometres away!

Some animals smell with different body parts. A male moth smells with its feathery antennae. It can smell a female moth more than a kilometre away.

Why does food smell good?

Food smells good when it is safe to eat.

Fresh fruit and vegetables smell lovely. They are healthy to eat. When food smells bad, it might not be safe to eat.

Do a blindfold smell test. Can you name different fruits just by their smell?

A hammerhead shark smells blood and food in the water. Its nostrils are long way apart on its strange head. This helps the shark to find where a smell is coming from.

Bees are attracted to flowers by their colour and smell. They feed on the flower's sweet nectar.

How do we taste?

We taste with our tongue,
but we use our nose as well.

Taste buds on our tongue tell us if food is sweet, sour, salty or bitter. But to get the full flavour we must smell food as we eat it.

Try a blindfold taste test. Can you guess the flavour of potato crisps from their taste? Now pinch your nose gently. Is it harder to guess the flavour when you cannot smell?

Some animals taste with other parts of their bodies. An octopus tastes with its tentacles. When it touches something that tastes good, it pulls it into its mouth.

A mosquito tastes with its feet. When a mosquito lands on a human, it tastes their skin before biting and sucking out blood.

How can I look after my senses?

You can look after your senses in many ways. If you don't, they can easily be damaged.

Be careful when you use sharp objects. Never push them into somebody's eyes, ears or nose.

When it is sunny, protect your skin with sun tan lotion and wear a hat to shade your face. Never look directly at the sun.

Wear a helmet when you cycle. If you fall without a helmet you might damage your brain. Our brains make sure all our senses work well.

How do you think these things could damage your senses: computer screens, loud music, television? What can you do to protect your senses from them?

27

Glossary

braille

A way of reading and writing. The letters are made from raised dots that a blind person can read by touch.

echo

A sound that bounces back to your ear. You can hear an echo when you clap near a cliff or in a cave.

nostrils

The two openings at the bottom of the nose. We breathe and smell though our nostrils.

prey

An animal that is hunted by another animal. When a fox hunts a rabbit, the rabbit is the fox's prey.

pupil

The black hole at the centre of the eye which lets in light.

sensitive

Something is sensitive when it can feel, or sense in another way.

sign language

A language spoken using hand movements instead of words.

taste buds

Small bumps on our tongue which send messages to our brain to tell us how our food tastes.

tentacle

A long, bendy part of the body. Some animals feel and smell with their tentacles.

Index

Animal index and quiz

Use your animal index to find the answers to this animal quiz!

- How many eyes do some spiders have?

- How does an aardvark use its ears to catch ants?

- How does a seal keep warm?

- A bear can smell honey from far away. How far?

- Which part of the body does an octopus use to taste?

- Which senses does a mole use to find its way around underground?